The Art of Coaching Youth Soccer

Match Related Drills and Exercises
for Fun and Winning

by Jason Carney

REEDSWAIN

**Library of Congress
Cataloging - in - Publication Data**

by Jason Carney
   The Art of Coaching Youth Soccer
   Match Related Drills and Exercises for Fun and Winning

ISBN No. 1-59164-027-X
Lib. of Congress Catalog No. 2002109728
© 2002

Editing
Bryan R. Beaver

Printed by
DATA REPRODUCTIONS
Auburn, Michigan

Reedswain Publishing
612 Pughtown Road
Spring City, PA 19475
800.331.5191
www.reedswain.com
info@reedswain.com

Table of Contents

iv

Introduction

I believe there is an art to coaching. Whoever you speak to , everyone will and should have an open opinion on soccer. As a coach you should accept criticism, if given in a positive spirit, and never think that you know everything. You should be looking for new ideas all the time and be creative in your sessions.

The coaching style you will read in this book is based on the belief that: 'Players learn more when having fun'.
The drills are fun and players can learn from them. Each coaching session should have an objective.

- It should be fun
- It should have a purpose
- That purpose should be achievable
- It should be match related and realistic
- It should involve teaching techniques and tactics
- It should be well organized and prepared

Coaching has improved dramatically over the past 10 years and the coaching sessions you put on are vital in how your team performs. Players should use each coaching session to improve and as a coach you should prepare each session with the learning process in mind.

It is not enough to have one or two favorite drills, players will become bored and lose interest. This book provides a variety of drills to help the coach organize training sessions that will allow players the opportunity to improve.
As a coach you must have rules. Never break those rules.
Players will respect a coach who is organized, disciplined, but most of all honest.

I am grateful to Gary Peters and Ged Starkey from Preston North End Centre of Excellence and also the people from Johnson Fold Estate who had a great passion for football.

Starting the Warm-Up

Before a game or a training session the muscles must be prepared for the demands that will be placed on them.

1. Get loose and warm with a slow jog, lasting 3-4 minutes.

2. Make huge circles with the arms to get the blood flowing to the upper body as well.

3. A slow jog backwards for 10-15 yards.

4. Side-steps, keep turning after 4 steps and wave both arms in the air.

5. Knee lifts. Lift the thigh up and slap it lightly with both hands, one after the other.

6. Get the players to perform exercises on the muscles they will use in a game. Kick out the legs, left leg to right hand, right leg to left hand. Kick legs out straight. For groins, jog and lift the knee and swing it outwards / inwards.

Increased blood flow to the muscles will warm them up, making them more elastic. You get a better stretch from a warm muscle. This reduces the risk of injury, so don't stretch when cold, get warm first.

Stretching

Players should stretch before and AFTER every match or training session. The coach must stress the importance of stretching to the players, especially the younger ones. After a game you can all go for a cool down and use this time to chat to the team about how you think they performed and what their strengths and weaknesses were. Stretching after a game prevents the risk of becoming stiff and sore.

It is important that the muscles to be used are stretched to their maximum length. A better stretch is possible if the muscle is relaxed beforehand. If a stretch starts to hurt, this is the body's warning that muscle damage may occur, so the muscle will involuntarily contract to protect itself, preventing a decent stretch.

- Perform all the movements that will be done in the game. This is the most effective warm up before a match.

- Stretch until a mild tension in the muscle is felt.

- If it hurts, ease off - over-stretching can cause strained muscles.

- Hold each stretch for 6-10 seconds and stretch each muscle group twice.

Make Warm-Ups Fun

After the warm up and stretching the players will find it more enjoyable if the next stage of the warm up is done with the ball. Below are some exercises that you can use in your sessions.

Skill Circuit in Twos

1 touch passing in small area using both feet

Long passing. Looking for quality pass & control.

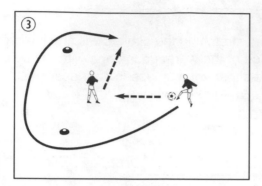

Player 1 passes to player 2 then runs around the cones & receives return pass from 2.
COMMUNICATION

1 touch passing through the cones using left foot (go both directions).

Kick ups. 1st man flicks ball up, 2nd man has 2 touches, then 3 then 4 etc.

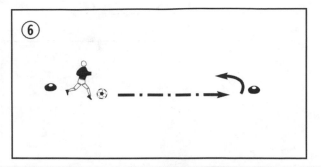

Dribble to each cone and perform a turn.

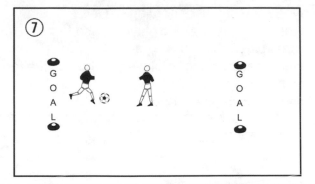

1 v 1. Getting to cones by dribbling
past opponent.

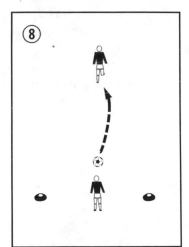

Throw-ins. Pass back
1st time or control &
back.

Skill Circuit in Threes

Player 2 Passes to oncoming player 1.
Player 1 sets the ball for player 2 and turns to run towards player 3.
Player 2 passes long to player 3 who passes to oncoming player 1.
Player 1 passes back and so on.

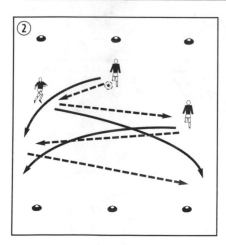

The middle man always starts the exercise. He can pass to the player to his left or right.
Once the players have passed the ball they follow it quickly, moving to the opposite side.
Then players come back the other way.

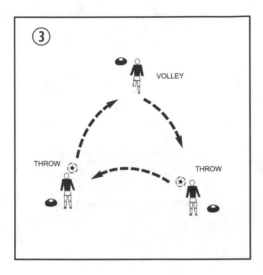

Players 1 & 3 hold a ball each in their hands.
Player 1 throws the ball for player 2 to volley.
Player 3 throws his ball for player 1 to catch.
Player 2 volleys ball for player 3 to catch.
Go the opposite way. Can also do headers.

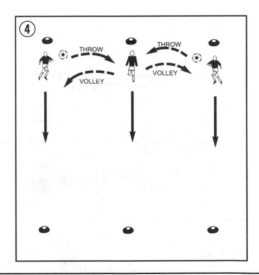

Players on the outside hold a ball.
Player 1 throws the ball for player 2 to volley back.
Player 2 is facing forward using right & left foot.
Player 3 then throws for player 2 to volley.
Once they reach the end line, swap the middle man.

Players on the outside pass to the player in the middle.
Player in the middle receives the ball in an open body position and passes to opposite player.
Player in the middle is limited to 3 touches.

Player 1 passes to player 2.
Player 3 shadows player 2.
Player 2 turns away from player 3 and dribbles to the cone.
Player 1 then moves up to shadow player 3.
Player 2 passes to player 3 who turns and dribbles to the other cone, and so on.
Concentrate on the players' turning technique.

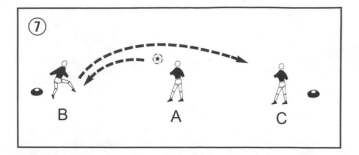

Player A throws the ball to player B.
Player B volleys the ball back for player A to catch.
Player A throws the ball back and player B volleys the ball over player A's head for player C to catch.
After player C catches the ball, player A moves to B, player B to C and player C to A.
Players use alternate feet, right foot to player A, left foot to player C.

Variations:
Players perform half volleys.
Players control with chest or thigh and pass back on the ground or as a volley.
Headers.

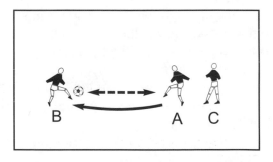

Player A passes one touch to Player B. Player A quickly moves to player B's position. Player B passes one touch to player C then moves to C's position, and so on.

Warm-Up as a Group

Separate your players into two teams and mark out a suitable area.

Put half the players on the outside with a ball each and the others in the middle.

Variations:

Players in the middle move around the pitch and when they receive a pass from a player on the outside, they pass back one touch.

Players in the middle take two touches and pass back.

Players on the outside throw the ball to a player's chest, who then controls it and passes back.

Players throw for headers and volleys.

Remove half of the balls. Players in the middle, once they have received a pass, pass to a player who doesn't have a ball.

Focus on:

- Communication
- Movement
- Quality of pass
- Shielding the ball

The Structure of :
AJAX F.C. AMSTERDAM

" If you see one Ajax team play, you have seen them all."

Ajax F.C. is a club that has been one of the major forces in European football for decades. Their success has come from the ability to produce home grown talent. The youth section is completely independent of the first team professionals, but all members of the club work closely together.
Ajax prefers to do things their way and has a club.
Memorandum for all staff members: You either do it the Ajax way or move on.

Each squad consists of:

◆ 2 Goalkeepers

◆ 4 Right footed players

◆ 4 Left footed players

◆ 3 players for middle of Defense / Midfield

◆ 3 players for Center forward

The club is allowed to sign young players who live within a 90 km radius (55 miles) of Amsterdam and use an interesting reverse acronym when assessing, teaching or scouting players.

T   Technique - No 1 requirement.
I   Intelligence - Essential for their style of play.
P   Personality - Important for a **TEAM** player.
S   Speed - Of thought and action.

Scouts are told to look for the reverse, S.P.I.T., because the club officials believe they have the ability to improve the intelligence and technique of the players once they are at the club.

During training and games parents are allowed to support but not interfere and are never allowed to shout advice. There is a sign at each session which REQUESTS SILENCE. Tennis balls and specially designed soft balls are used regularly,　especially at the younger age groups. This improves the touch and technique. Small sided games, 4 v 4, are played to teach the diamond and triangle shapes which are a part of Ajax play.

Training is interval based and covers the following areas:

Ball Control - Dribbling, passing, moving etc.
Duels - 1 v 1, co-defending, defensive heading etc, sense of position
Athletic capabilities - Start speed, speed over 10m & 30m +, agility, staying running and jumping power.
Charisma - Creativity, team spirit etc.

The under 17 & 18s train together. The sessions include the goalkeepers, defenders, midfield players and forwards working in separate groups, each with a coach specializing in their field of play.

Each week the training session includes a half hour for improving running technique. All groups do thorough warm ups and cool downs after training and matches and this is the culture of Holland. In Britain we must add this to our training program at all levels, so that in the future it will become natural for our players to prepare properly.

Footwork drills and conditioning circuits are included from the age of 8 through senior level:

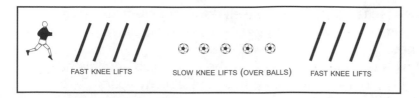

FAST KNEE LIFTS   SLOW KNEE LIFTS (OVER BALLS)   FAST KNEE LIFTS

This exercise is part of a warm-up and it concentrates on running technique. It is not quantity that matters but quality. Running over the poles doing the fast knee lifts gets the players to stay upright and pumping their arms as they are lifting their knees. When approaching the balls slow down and concentrate on getting your knees over the balls. You can use different steps in the fast part :

- 1 foot in facing forwards
- 2 feet in facing forwards
- 1 foot in facing sideways
- 2 feet in facing sideways

A soccer player's speed and agility depend largely on his running coordination. However, running technique is an area that is too often ignored in the youth training program today. A systematic but fun running training program is crucial to developing better players.

What can we learn from Ajax?

The thing to remember from this section is that Ajax produces some quality home grown talent. Ajax has, and I believe every club should have, a policy going right through the club of what they expect from their players and coaches. Every coach in the club, whether it be for the first team, the reserves or youth team, should follow a structured coaching policy. Because opinions on how soccer should be played vary, if you don't have a structure things can be difficult.

For example, a player could break through to the first team as a right full back, having been told by his youth coaches that he cannot cross the half way line and must concentrate only on defending. Unfortunately, the way the first team plays is with imagination and flair, so now this player has a problem fitting into the team.

All coaches at clubs should sit down and discuss a formula on how to improve players. This will help both the players and the coaches.

Ajax has a running school for the entire club and this has been a basic principle of their training for many years.
Another thing to add to your training sessions are running techniques. Later on in the book you will come across different exercises and drills on this topic.

Here are 5 items that will ultimately lead to success:

      1. HARD WORK
      2. DISCIPLINE.
      3. ORGANIZATION.
      4. QUALITY.
      5. SPIRIT.

Better Running Technique, Better Soccer

What's the point ?

Nowadays, soccer is more competitive than ever before. Every team must try to improve in every department, and running is no exception.

The teams that are successful are the teams that are organized and disciplined. You need look no further than Manchester United to see what can be achieved by having set rules for players. Every team can be a Manchester United in its own league if things are done properly.

Coaches should not be reluctant to bring in running technique as part of their training program. If by coaching the technique of running you can make your players that little bit quicker, then you will have an edge on other teams who don't address this issue.

A soccer player's speed depends on his running coordination. For this reason, running coordination exercises are crucial. A player who can control his running can perform at a higher level. It's a matter of directing muscular impulses more precisely between the muscular and the nervous system. Muscles must be able to cope with all kinds of movement in running.

It is important to remember that motivation plays a big part in running exercises, so be inventive, and don't put the same exercises on week in and week out. Once you have added the running exercises to your training, keep them there. Given all the demands on soccer players, running exercises are crucial.

As a coach you must be aware of the need for coordination programs because many players are under-developed in this area. A lot of Professional clubs now have their youth players doing the running techniques as part of the session and you have to emphasize the importance of the running exercises. Below are some running exercises to try. But remember, young players learn best when they are engaged by the exercises and having fun, so try to be creative and make the exercises challenging and fun.

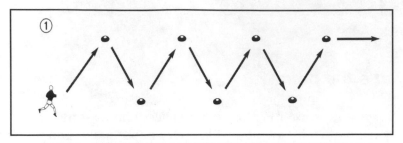

Players sprint cone to cone with lots of small steps.
a) Players sprint one cone, jog the next.
b) Sprint one cone, backwards slowly the next.
c) Put a ball on each cone and players must knock the ball off.

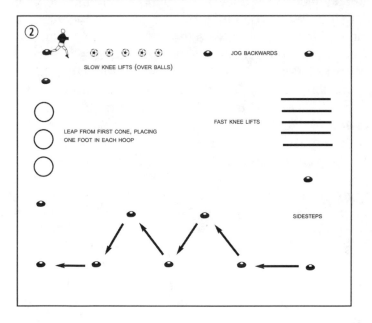

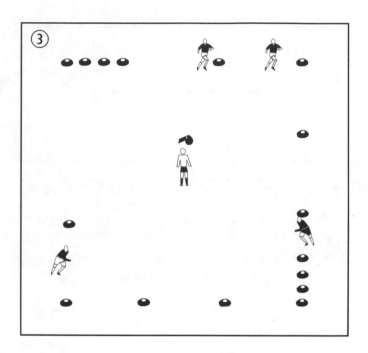

Coordination.
Set up cones around a square 20 x 20.
2 sets of 5 cones 5 yards apart.
2 sets of 5 cones 1 yard apart.
The players jog around the square and when they get to the cones that are 5 yards apart they go around each one sideways. Players shuffle around the cones looking at the coach.
When the players get to the cones that are 1 yard apart they go sideways in and out of the cones, lifting their head to look at the coach.

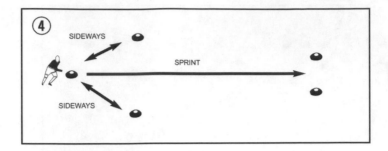

Each player runs sideways to the first cone, then to the second cone, then sprints to the gate.
Players must touch the cones.
Variation:
Add 2 players at the cones, holding a ball. The runner moves sideways and volleys/heads the ball back.

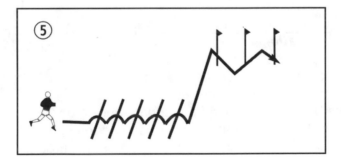

Players perform fast knee lifts over poles then zigzag in and out of the flags and sprint to the end line.
Players perform different steps over the poles:
Forward - one step in.
Forward - two steps in.
Sideways - one step in.
Sideways - two steps in.

The ABC's of Running

SPRINT DRILL WARM-UP

After a full stretching routine this is a warm up program to perform before the sprint drills commence.
Set out a 20 yard track and the players perform each exercise to the end of the track and jog back to the start.

- Side to side skipping on the left side.

- Side to side skipping on the right side.

- High knee lifts - Raise the thighs quickly.

- Fast knee lifts - Don't lift knees as high as normal knee lifts.

- Flick legs up behind.

- Cross over legs on the left side.

- Cross over legs on the right side.

- Heels to hands in between legs.

- Heels to hands outside the legs.

- Skipping - The take off leg should be completely extended at the hip, knee and foot at the apex of the jump.

SPRINT DRILLS

SNAP UPS - Jog, but every few paces right knee snaps up to 90 degree angle. The important part is the speed of the snap. Head must be still and focusing ahead. Make sure the arms are pumping. How quickly this exercise is done is unimportant, the speed of the snap and technique are what matters. Repeat with left knee.

SNAP UPS BEHIND - Slow jog but every few paces snap up the right heel to hit the buttock. Repeat with left heel.

SNAP SKIPPING - This time work each leg alternately. A slow jog then snap skip one leg after the other lifting the knees. Keep the head still, eyes looking ahead and pump the arms.

HEEL FLICKS - Alternate heel to buttocks.

HIGH KNEE RAISE - On the spot have players perform high knee lifts. Get them pumping their arms and lifting their knees at right angles, as if they are standing on hot ashes. On shout of "go", they sprint to the end.

TECHNIQUE - Sprinting full out but concentrating on technique. Head still, eyes focused ahead, arms pumping up and down, not side to side, and upright body position.

THE SPRINT - Slow jog looking straight ahead. On the signal, players sprint to the end, concentrating on all the techniques.

MAKE SURE TO DO A COOL DOWN AT THE END OF EACH SESSION

The need for SPEED

The importance of SPEED

The first thing most managers will ask when being told about a player is, "Is he fast?".

Soccer speed is the ability to start quickly from all different positions, accelerate to top speed in the shortest time possible, change direction, and stop rapidly under control to make the play.

Players are either born with speed or not, but by doing the right exercises you can certainly make a player faster.
In track, the difference between winning and losing is often down to milliseconds, this is why every effort is made trying to get a runner from A to B as quickly and efficiently as possible.

Teaching sprinting technique in soccer is a different proposition. Soccer is multi-directional, and even if a player was taught the correct techniques, in a game situation all that would be forgotten as the player runs for the ball.
Correct sprinting techniques would not make a player quicker by any significant amount, so training for speed of reaction and agility is much more important.

The ability to sprint is essential, but also crucial is the ability to turn at speed. Mixing these two ingredients will improve a player's 'soccer speed'.

REACTION SPRINTS

These are exercises to sharpen the body's reaction times. It is important to remember that rest is also important in sprinting. For players to benefit from sprints they must be quite fresh, so have them walking back and give them time to recover. The quality of the run is important, not the quantity. Below are some starting positions, sprint for 10 yards:

◆   Push-up position.

◆   Lying face down, hands behind the head.

◆   Lying face up, hands on stomach.

◆   Kneeling with hands behind the head.

◆   Kneeling on one knee.

◆   On hands and knees, facing forward & backward

◆   Lying on your side.

◆   Doing an imaginary header before sprinting.

Use a whistle or clap to start off the sprints.

Get real.........

As a coach you have to think of your players' capabilities, and look after them the best way possible. When you are doing a sprinting session, remember that rest is vital, so don't over-do the sprinting.

The sprints should be done over a 15 to 20 yard distance.

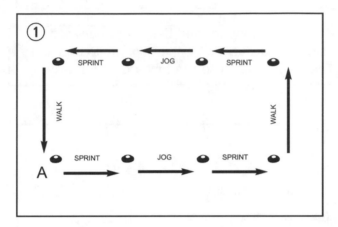

After a good warm-up, cones are set out 15 yards apart as shown above. Players line up in pairs at A. They complete the circuit 5 times. This is a good exercise as it is match related. Players will feel the benefits of this session as opposed to going on a long run.

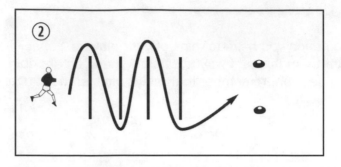

Player runs forward and backward between
poles using little steps, then sprints to end line.
The player may also run forward all the way.

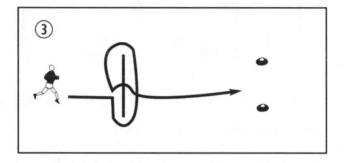

Player runs small steps around pole and sprints
to end line.

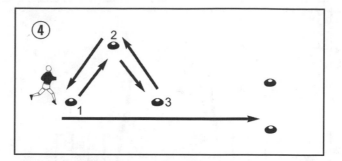

Player runs with small steps forward to cone 2. He then goes backward to cone 3, around 3, forward to cone 2, backward to cone 1 and sprints through gate.

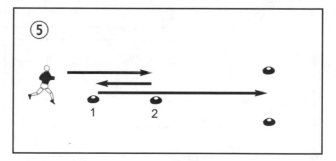

1. Player runs to cone 2, backward to cone 1 and then sprints to end.
2. Player does a figure 8 around both cones and sprints to end line.

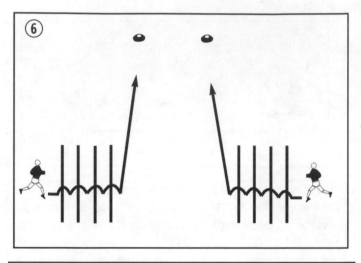

Players perform fast knee lifts over poles, turn and sprint to cones

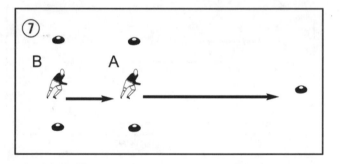

Cones are set out 3 yards apart, with another cone a further 15 yards away.
The players get in two's, facing each other.
Both players slowly move side to side to cones.
Player A is the one who sets off the sprint. Once he goes, player B has to try to tag him.
Variation:
Players pass a ball one touch to each other until player A decides to go.

Better Footwork

Push & Go - The partner pushes against the sprinter leaning forward; at some point, the hold is released and the player sprints forward.

Quick Foot Ladder - The footwork drills are only limited to one's imagination. The ladder is made up of 8 or more 18 inch connected segments.
run straight through with specific steps required, such as:
- Steps in every square.
- 2 steps in every square.
- Side-steps in every square.
- 2 side-steps in every square.
- Sprint to the ladder, quick step through, sprint out.
- Side steps, missing a square out each time.

Dot Drill - Think of the 5 dots on a die. The dots are numbered 1 (bottom right), 2 (center), 3 (bottom left), 4 (top left), 5 (top right). Right foot starts on 1, the left foot is on 3. Using R as a notation for right foot and L as the left foot, the sequence is R-2, L-3, R-4, L-2, R-1, L-3. This sequence is executed as many times as possible in a 15-30 second time period. The next sequence is the same, only with the left foot starting. The movement should imitate a forward movement of steps, followed by a backward run of two steps. Hopscotch with turns can also be used with the dots. The dots could be spray painted or just imagined.

Low Hurdles - Start the hurdles (6-8 inches high) about 2-3 feet apart. As the players improve, move them closer together. Note, always RUNOUT after the last hurdle.
- one step run through
- two steps between each hurdle
- go sideways
- incorporate more speed with a run up to the hurdles

Low Box Quick Step - use a low box (4-6 inches high) to step on and off.

'Lets do the twist'...

Here are some exercises that will help your players improve their agility, twisting and turning.
All these exercises should be done at 90% maximum speed.

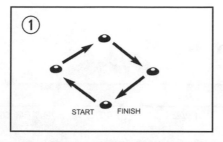

| Touch or run around each marker |

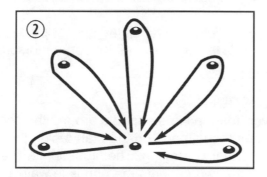

| Touch or run around each marker |

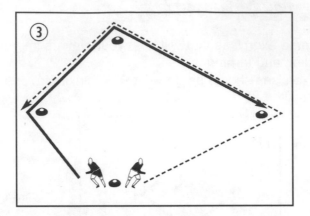

Two players stand at the starting line facing opposite directions.
On the coaches command:
Each player sprints around each cone and back to
the start.
Each player sprints around all the cones. Once they
get back home they go around the cone and sprint
the opposite way.

Get the players in two's:
One player from each pair sprints around the cones.
Their partner then stands on the start facing the
way their partner is running. The first sprinter then
tags his partner who sprints the opposite way, and
back to the finish.

To make the turning more precise, place balls on
top of the cones. Players who knock a ball off are
disqualified.

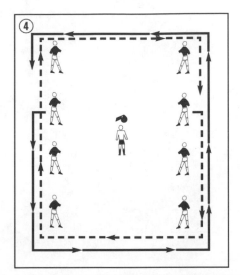

Players stand facing each other, five yards apart.
The coach calls out a player's name. That person and the
player opposite sprint around the players and back to
where they started.
If the players are running and the coach shouts 'Turn', the
players have to change direction and return to the start.

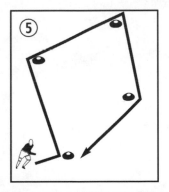

Touch each cone with foot

Pre-Season Training

Endurance and Stamina

Stamina is very important in a game. You need to maintain energy levels and concentration throughout the match. A player may have good technical ability, but if he's not fit he will struggle against a fit player, even one with lesser skill.

It only takes a second to score a goal, whether it be the first or last minute. It can make the difference between winning and losing.

For the first few sessions pick a route, ideally over grass with hills. Try to change each route so players are not doing the same run time after time. Set the run at 3 miles and alternate between jogging and running at 75% of top speed (this is game related). Pick markers such as trees, paths, lamp posts etc. When doing this, make sure players jog, it is important to get a breather. When players get back from this run, don't give them more running exercises, get the ball out and do some drills or use this time for shooting practice.

REST IS AN IMPORTANT PART OF THE TRAINING PROGRAM. DON'T OVERDO IT!

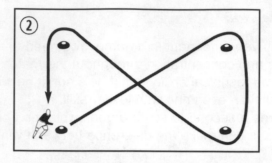

Make your own area or use a full size pitch.

Set players off in 3's or 4's and time each group.
After the first rep use the fastest time as a motivator.
For every second over the fastest time, each group
must do 5 push-ups.
Once all the groups are back, stop the clock.
Do 3 sets of 3 repetitions and rest for about one
minute between each rep and 2 minutes between
each set.

The Beep Test

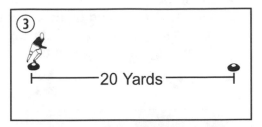

(3)

20 Yards

The beep test is a great way to build stamina through the season. If you train outside in the winter the beep test really gets the players warmed up and ready for the drills ahead.
A good way to keep the players motivated and to watch their fitness level improve is to analyze their performance. Make a chart and note what level each player reaches. Don't do the test every week as players will become bored. In amateur soccer, getting players to practice is difficult, so make sessions interesting and enjoyable.
The first 5 levels are easy, so let the players dribble the ball for these early stages.
When the players reach the end lines, they must not turn until the beep, so make it clear at the start that players must pace themselves.
After the beep test is finished, get the players to have another stretch and take some fluids as the test is very demanding. The players will be tired, so this is a good time to do some ball work. Don't go into more running exercises, the players need time to recover.

Stations

A good way to keep the players on their toes and keep the spirit going is station training. Depending on how many players you are coaching you can set up a number of stations where the players can work on technique, teamwork and team spirit.

Play 1 v 1 through 4 v 4
Play with one bounce or no bounces.
Limit each player to 2 touches

X's play two touch and keep possession.
Players on the outside cannot pass to each other.
Whoever gives the ball away changes with O and becomes a defender.
To make it more difficult, put three defenders in the middle (the coach can join in.)

Player dribbles to gate and shoots at goal.

Player passes ball forward then runs and shoots.

Coach stands at gate and player dribbles around him and shoots.

Player chips ball to coach's hands. Coach throws ball up for player to volley.

Player juggles ball to cones and volleys at goal.

Coach stands at the side of the goal with the balls. He passes to the player, who controls the ball and shoots.

Goalkeeper can throw the ball for the player to control and shoot.

Goalkeeper rolls ball towards cones and the player shoots 1st time.

Player runs to 1st cone and back, 2nd cone and back and so on.

Player does the same as first exercise but when he gets to cone 5 he goes back to cone 4 then back to 5, to 3 back to 5, to 2 back to 5 etc.

Player sprints to cone 2 and jogs slowly backwards to 1, then sprints to 3 and backwards to 2 then 4 to 3 and 5 to 4 then sprints past 5 and walks back.

Same exercise as above but when player has sprinted to 5 he goes to 3 and backwards to 4, then 2 backwards to 3 until he gets back to the start.

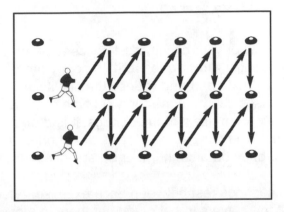

Player sprints diagonally to cone then jogs to his left. When he gets to the next cone he sprints diagonally again until he gets to the end, then he walks back.

Same as above but when player gets to cone 5 he works his way back to the start, sprinting diagonally and jogging across.

Players run diagonally left and right to the end as shown with dashed lines.

Players run same as exercise 7 but also come back diagonally to the start.

Fitness Circuit

The structure of your circuit must concentrate on quality, rather than quantity. **Don't overdo it!** A poorly organized circuit can overload a body part and reduce the quality in the exercise.

The exercises can be done for a set time or for a set number of reps. If your team has various abilities, it is probably best to use time, but if you think some players are short on motivation, making everybody do a set number of reps gives each player a target.

Take 15 seconds rest between each exercise. Alternatively you can put the players in pairs and get them to move from one exercise to another, doing a different   exercise at each station.

JOGGING ON THE SPOT.......1 Min
PUSH-UPS.........................20 Reps
HEADERS ON THE SPOT......30 Sec
SIT UPS.............................20 Reps
BURPEES............................20 Reps
SQUAT THRUSTS.................20 Reps
RUNNING 3/4 PACE...............1 Min
COORDINATION EXERCISES......1 Min.
STRETCHING EXERCISES..........1 Min

Shoot on Sight

Shooting sessions should be game related and focused on technique. They should also be suited to the ability of your players. Start the session easy and gradu-ally build up to more difficult exercises.

- The technique should be clean and players should concentrate on hitting the target.

- Players often lash at the ball. Get them to relax and follow through with the shot.

- Players should practice shooting with both feet.

- Successful finishing creates confidence, so if the exercises are not working be patient and keep working on technique.

- To make the sessions effective, have players in two groups shooting at 2 goals. This will keep players from getting bored and the more practice they have the better they will become.

Running Technique and Shooting Warm-Up

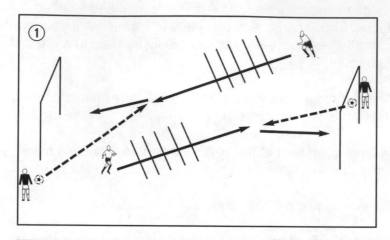

Player does fast knee lifts over poles. Coach throws ball for player to volley / head at goal.

Variation: Same as above but the coach rolls ball along the ground for player to shoot.

After a few goes, get players to go the opposite way so that they use both feet.

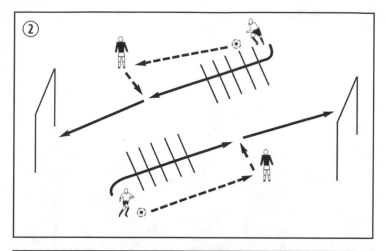

Player passes ball down the side of the poles to coach then performs fast knee lifts over poles. Coach passes ball into player's path for him to shoot.

Player chips the ball into coach's hands, who then throws ball in the air for Player to volley.

Player passes the ball along the side of the poles, performs fast knee lifts and shoots at goal.
Concentrate on the weight of the pass.

The players can perform different steps over the poles: fast knee lifts sideways, putting two steps in between each pole, etc.
This is a good session to get the players warmed up for the shooting session.
Before the players start to strike the ball, make sure they have done a good warm up and stretched.

Shooting Technique
Practice Makes Perfect

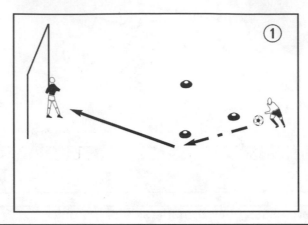

With a large group of players and the right equipment, shooting exercises can be interesting and
fun, while still concentrating on technique. Players
must concentrate on striking the ball with the
laces part of the boot. Tell them to relax and follow through on contact, don't lash out at the ball.
Gradually build up the exercises to more difficult
drills.

Players dribble to line and shoot at goal.
Players pass ball forward to line, then run and
shoot.
Players juggle ball to line then volley at goal.
Players dribble to right hand cone and shoot.
Players dribble to left hand cone and shoot. Get
players to shoot across the goalkeeper.
Same as 4 & 5 but coach stands on left cone.
Player must dribble to right cone and shoot before
coach tackles him (do alternate cones). Players
must take less touches if they want to get their
shot on goal.

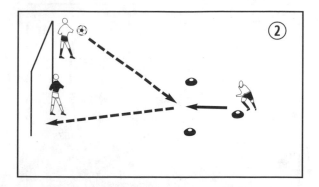

Coach stands behind goal and serves ball for player to shoot.

Player takes one touch out of his feet and shoots.
Player takes ball to left or right cone and shoots across goalkeeper.
Players get in two's. One player controls the ball and passes it forward for his partner to shoot.

Coach can choose different passes for players to deal with.

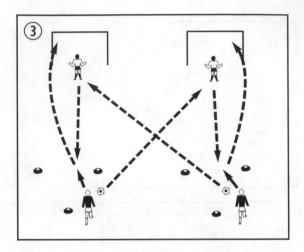

Players cross the ball to the opposite goalkeepers.

Goalkeeper throws the ball out to the player who controls and shoots.
Goalkeeper rolls the ball out and the player shoots first time.
Be sure to concentrate on technique.

Shooting Games

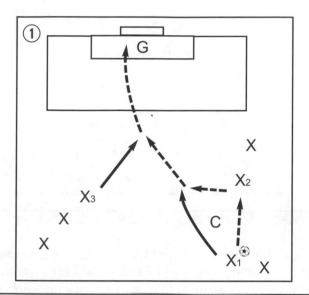

X1 plays a 1– 2 around the coach with X2.
X1 passes ball for X3 to run onto.
X3 takes one touch and shoots at goal.
Players rotate after completing an exercise, X1
goes to X3, X3 to X2 and X2 to X1.
Focus on:
Quality of passing
Communication
Timing of run
Technique of shot
Variation:
Make exercise all one touch
Add a defender, and play 2 v 1. X1 can play to
front man or pass to man on back post.
Play 3 v 2. X1 joins in the attack.

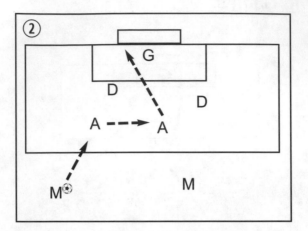

Attackers & Defenders play 2 v 2 in the penalty box.
The aim of the exercise is for the Attackers to create an opening to shoot by using their movement. If there is no opportunity to shoot, the Attackers can pass back to the midfielders and start again.

Focus on:
Quality of passing - Movement -
Communication - Decision (shot or pass) -
Technique of shot.

In a 40 x 30 playing area 2 teams play 5 v 5.

Both teams play free play and shoot whenever they get an opportunity.

Variations:
Play two touch.
Each team completes 3 passes or more before a shot.
The 3rd pass has to be a shot.
Each team has 15 seconds to score

Between the Sticks

It is difficult for coaches to involve goalkeepers in their training programs. The problem is how to make goalkeeper training part of our practice sessions. An ideal solution is a goalkeeper coach who works separately from the outfield players and concentrates on the attributes of goalkeepers.

It is important to plan sessions that involve the goalkeepers, but having a goalkeeper coach makes life easier and keeps the goalkeepers interested.

The main areas for goalkeepers to concentrate on are:

Technique - picking up & catching balls - punching - passing with hand or foot - diving - jumping - recovering - control on back passes.
Tactics - organizing players - positional sense - command goal area - set pieces.
Fitness - Mobility - coordination - endurance - flexibility.
Psychology - concentration - positive attitude - bravery - confidence - stability.

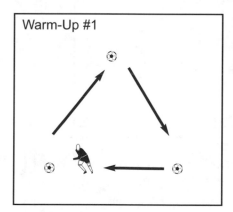

Warm-Up #1

The GK moves around the triangle and dives on each ball.
Work for 30 seconds.
Go the other way.
Focus on:
Technique of diving on the ball.

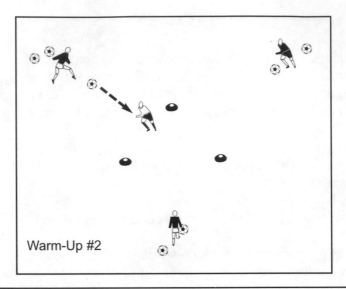

Warm-Up #2

The GK moves around the triangle saving shots from the players on the outside.
Work all GKs for 40 seconds then after a rest period go the opposite way.

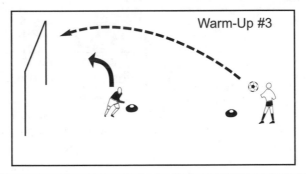

Warm-Up #3

Goalkeeper jogs out to cone.
When he gets to the cone the coach tries to throw the ball over the goalkeeper to score.
Focus on:
Recovery after throw.
Technique - catching / diving.
Decision - catch or tip over cross bar.

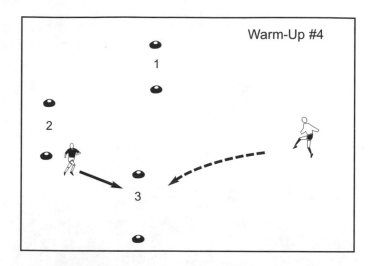

The coach calls 1,2 or 3. The Goalkeeper runs to that goal and saves the coach's shot.

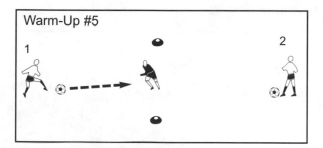

Player 1 shoots at Goalkeeper.
Goalkeeper tries to make a save, recovers quickly and makes a save from player 2.
Have plenty of balls ready.
Goalkeepers save ten shots then rest or change keepers.

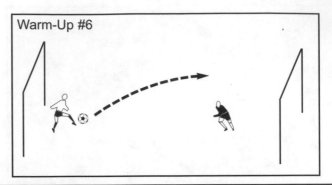

Warm-Up #6

A 1 v 1 competition for goalkeepers.
Goalkeepers can score any way possible: throw, kick, drop kick.
As soon as one makes a save he can shoot.
Have plenty of balls ready.
Focus on:
Technique of throwing, kicking and saving.
Angles and getting set.

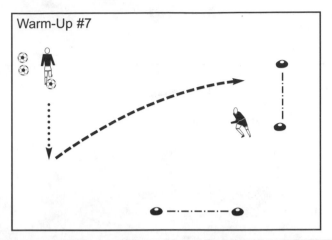

Warm-Up #7

Player 1 dribbles down the wing and tries to score in either goal.
Goalkeeper must defend both goals.
If a goal is scored the new keeper comes in.
If the goalkeeper cannot reach the ball he must shout away.
Focus on:
Ideal for working on the keeper's ability to cover the near post shot, as well as cutting off crosses.

To keep the GK on his toes, add an attacker.

GK takes crosses at the highest point.

All Together Now
Goalkeeping and Shooting

Player 1 crosses for GK to catch.
GK rolls ball to player 2.
Player 2 controls ball and shoots at goal.
GK
Focus on:
Positional play - catching - distribution
Forward Focus on:
crossing - shooting technique.

Player 1 crosses for players to finish first time with header or shot.
Player 2 passes for players to control, dribble and shoot.

Variations: Player 1. Add defender to cut out crosses.
Add extra attacker.
Player 2. Pass on ground for player to shoot first time.
Players get in two's, one controls and passes for teammate to shoot at goal.

Player 1 passes to Player 2 who stops the ball and makes his run.

Player 1 runs to the ball and passes to Player 3.

Player 1 makes his run into the box.

Player 3 stops ball for Player 4 to run and cross.

Focus on:

Quality of passing.

Because Player 2 has set off first, he attacks near post and Player 1 attacks far post.

Player 4 lifts his head and crosses.

To make the exercise easier, add cones for Players 1 & 2 to run around and for Player 4 to cross through.

Important:

Player 2 runs quickly to the cone.

He then slows down and looks to see if the ball is ready to be crossed.

As Player 4 is crossing the ball, Player 2 attacks the near post.

After passing, Player 1 runs quickly to the cone. He then hangs back ready to attack the far post.

Player 4 crosses to space and not to the man. This makes it easier for the attacker to make good contact with the ball.

Mastermind

The whole idea of coaching is to let the players think. As a coach you should build a picture inside the players' heads of the things you want them to do. So by being creative and making sure your drills are realistic you can have a big effect on developing your players. Players should be encouraged to solve problems themselves, with a little help from the coach of course.

One of the coach's main aims should be to develop not just players who are technically sound, but also players who are thinking players, players who can decide in an instant what to do and what technique to use.

Decision making is vital in a soccer player so it is important for players to observe and analyze what is happening. It is also important that you as a coach encourage the players.

Techniques can always be improved upon, but the more difficult task is coaching tactical insight. Many coaches believe you have to be born with tactical insight, and I agree to a certain point, but I also believe that with the right coaching exercises you can get the right results. I have experienced this with the youth teams I have coached. Yes, they are already talented players, but if a player is having fun training he will learn quickly.

The exercises you are about to read are designed to turn your players into **'THE THINKERS'**.

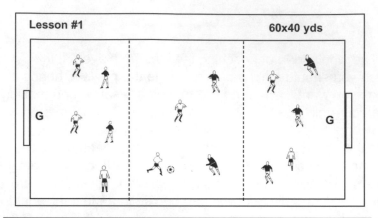

Lesson #1   **60x40 yds**

8 V 8 with goalkeepers.
3 players in the back third.
2 players in the middle third.
2 players in the front third.

The ball is started with one of the goalkeepers, who
throws the ball to a defender.
Once a pass has been made to a midfielder, one of the
defenders joins in the middle third and plays 3 v 2.
Once a midfielder passes to a forward, one of the mid-
fielders joins in with the attack, playing 3 v 3.
Once possession is lost the defending team must get
back to the formation of 3-2-2.
Variation:
Defenders have to make 5 passes before passing to
midfield.
Midfielders are only allowed two touches.
Goals can only be scored from a lay off by a forward.

See if the players can work out who should join in the
attack.

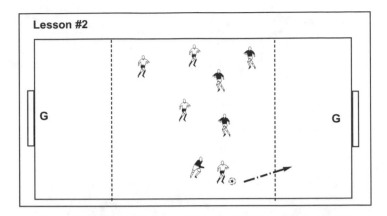

Lesson #2

A miniature field is made inside a full size soccer field. Two teams play 8 v 8.

The idea of the exercise is for players to choose when and when not to attack.

Game 1

A team can only score when one of its players gets the chance to dribble out of the box. The player who does this then plays a 1 v 1 against the goalkeeper.

Variation:

Add a defender to protect the goalkeeper.

Players now have to get past the defender and the goalkeeper.

Game 2

8 v 8, no defenders.

To score, players have to pass the ball into the zone for a teammate to run onto. Player cannot enter zone until the pass is made. He then plays a 1 v 1 with the Goalkeeper.

Variation:

Players shoot first time from pass.

Lesson #3 - Heading

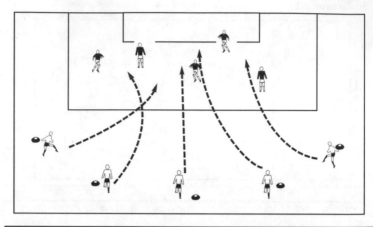

Heading is one topic of coaching that too often gets ignored. As you are developing the 'THINKING' player, here are some exercises on heading to build the picture in the players' heads.

The game is played in half the field. 5 v 5.

5 players spread out in the penalty box, the other 5 stand at the cones with 2 balls each.

Each player takes a turn chipping the ball in the box. The defenders try to stop them from scoring and also stop the ball from bouncing.

Focus on:

Making the right decision on the clearance.

Communication.

Lesson #4 - Pass and Move

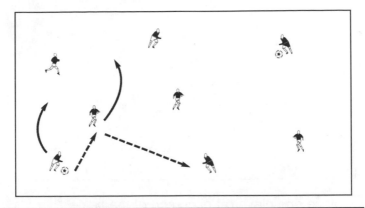

8 Players with two balls on a field 40 x 20 yards.
1. Players spread out and play two touch passing.
Once a player has passed he moves to another
space.

2. Players receive the pass on the move. The player
has to realize that the pass is on for him to receive,
then he must call for the pass to be made.

3. Play one touch.
Make sure players are scanning around to see where
the other players are.
Don't be predictable in the pass, change direction.
Use all varieties of passes.

4. One of the players puts on a bib.
Same as above, but if you pass to the player with the
bib you must receive a pass back from him straight
away.
Pass and explode.
Good communication.

64

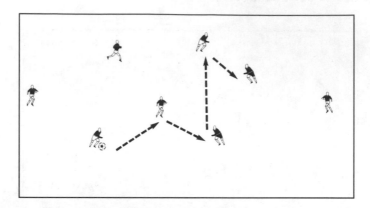

Now place one player at each end of the field.

Players pass one touch from one end to the other.
Once the players have passed to the end player, he
passes back for them to move to the other end.
Pass short and long.
Vary passes.
Be clever and alert

Variation:
Player who passes to the end player takes his place.
Put in a defender behind each end player..
No more than 4 passes to reach the end.
One of the players in the middle becomes a defender.
Be clever and alert.

Focus on:
Decision making, good communication, team play,
quality first touch.

Lesson #5 - Pass and Move 2

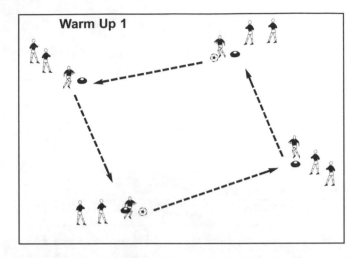

Some clubs are limited to the use of equipment, but it is important, if possible, to spend on the right equipment. Here are some drills that don't require a lot of equipment.

This drill can be used as part of a warm-up. Start with 2 balls at opposite corners and pass around the square using 2 touches. After passing, follow the pass and move to the next corner. After a few goes, go the opposite way.

Keep the drill tight to the cones and receive the ball with an open body position. Use different techniques to move the ball: take ball inside with left foot and pass with right, put in a feint, take ball outside of right foot and pass with right foot, etc..

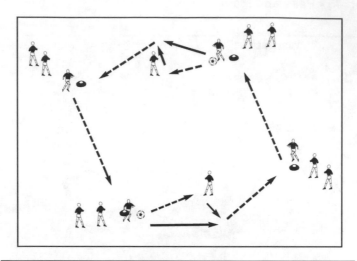

After 10 minutes add 2 players.
Now the players play a one two with the player in the middle.
Variation:
Players in the middle play as passive defenders. The player who receives the ball dribbles around the defender and passes to next player.
Players who pass the ball still follow their pass.
Put four players in the middle and play one twos around the square with 2 balls.
Focus on:
Communication
First touch
Pass
Body position

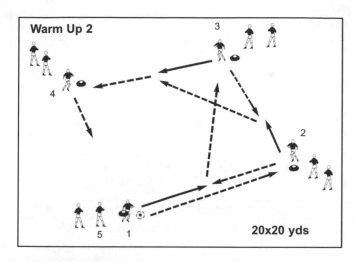

Warm Up 2

3

4

2

5   1   20x20 yds

Player 1 passes to 2
2 passes back to 1
Player 1 passes to 3
3 passes to incoming 2
2 passes ball into space for 3 to run onto
Player 3 passes to 4
Player 4 passes to 5
Players move around to each corner after passing.

Concentrate on one touch passing and get the players to communicate. Get them to concentrate on the weight of the pass and keep them interested and motivated. Vary the exercise by putting a goal in place of player 4. When player 2 passes to 3 he can shoot at goal.
Warm-ups are not all about running for 30 minutes, so as a coach you have to be creative. After a 5 minute jog and stretch, bring in the ball. After 5 minutes have the players do more stretching exercises.

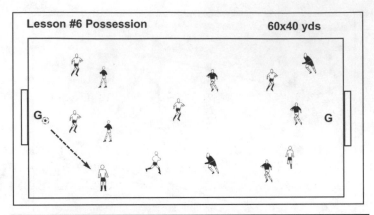

Lesson #6 Possession　　　　　　　**60x40 yds**

The game is played in an area 60 x 40.
8 v 8 or any decent number of players.
The game starts with one of the goalkeepers throwing the ball to one of his teammates.
Once a team scores a goal, it can only keep posses-sion (they can't score) until the other team scores.
Once the other team scores the game returns to nor-mal with both teams trying to score.
The team that is one goal ahead at the end of the session is the winner.
If the teams are level, play can either continue until a goal is scored or decide the game with penalty kicks.
Play two touch depending on the players' abilities.

DEFENDING

The Building Block of Soccer

Every game is won or lost in 1 v 1 situations. *If each player wins his 1 v 1s, you will win the match.*

Players should become confident in dealing with 1 v 1 situations on match day so in your training program you must include regular 1 v 1 situations. This is vital to both   individual and team success.

Encourage your defenders to:

- When to mark tight, when to mark loose.
- Keep an eye on:
    1. Your position.
    2. The ball.
    3. Your man.
    4. Possible passes.
- Make the right decision.
    1. Get to the ball first.
    2. Put pressure on your opponent
       while he is trying to control the ball.
    3. Stop your player from turning.
    4. When to make the tackle.
    5. When to win the header.
    6. When to clear the ball and when to pass.

Confidence in defending the 1v1 is vital to success and is ultimately up to the player's ability, attitude and technique.

The Basics

Player 1 passes to player 2.
Player 2 tries to pass the ball to player 4 while player 3 defends.

Focus on:
Marking tight, marking loose.
When to make the tackle.
Don't let the player turn.

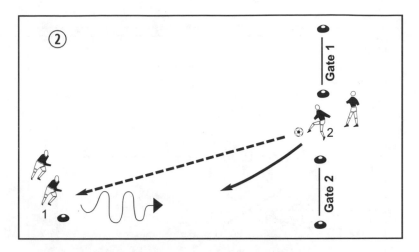

Without the ball. The coach shouts 1 or 2 and player 2 tries to run through that gate. Player 1 tries to tag him.
With the ball. Player 1 passes to player 2. Coach shouts 1 or 2. Player 2 tries to pass through that gate. Player 1 tries to stop the pass.
Same as above but player 2 tries to dribble through the gate
Player 1 must be confident in the challenge. Work on key factors.

Drills for Defending

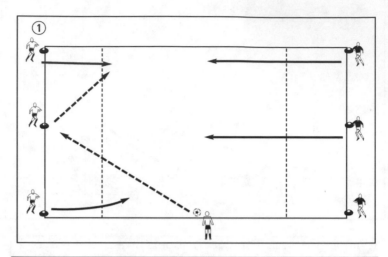

The coach passes the ball to the attackers who play 3 v 2 against the defenders.

Players must dribble into or make a pass to a team-mate in the area marked.

The overload of attackers means the defenders must cover for each other.

Go to 3 v 3. Get players to be positive and win their 1 v 1.

Use the key factors on defending.

Soccer is about opinions and coaches have different views on how they want their team to defend, so put your own ideas into all the defending drills.

1. The white team has five attacks at the black team.

When the team defending wins the ball the game has finished and the goalkeeper for the attacking team starts the drill again, until all five balls have been used.
After five attacks change over.
See how many goals are scored in the five attacks.

2. If the defending team wins the ball they can go and attack, but if the attackers win the ball back the game has finished.

3. The coach gives the defenders a player to mark on the attacking team.
A defender whose attacker scores does ten push-ups.

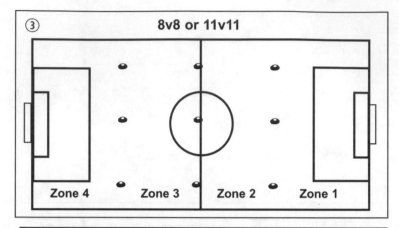

A regular 11v11 or 8 v. 8 game. Break the field into 4 horizontal zones. Award the defending team points when they win the ball back in a chosen zone. For example, the team might be given 3 points for winning the ball back in the first zone, two points for the second zone, one point for the third zone and no points for the fourth zone. This can change depending on where the coach wants the team to try to force the play.

Focus on:

Try to get the players to work together, collectively, as a unit, with all 11 players aware of the defensive plan. Can the defending team control the attacking team, making them play the ball in a certain area of the field, and then win the ball there?
Make sure you give all the key points on defending.
Make sure both teams are positive.

The object of this exercise is to work on the center-halves.
The players on the four cones are numbered.
The coach shouts a number and that player delivers the ball to the forwards.
The two defenders try to win the ball.
The forwards can pass back to server.

Focus on:
When to mark tight and when to mark loose.
When to win the tackle.
When the defenders win the ball, they can pass to any of the servers.
Also work on the forwards.

Variation:
Once a player on the outside has passed to the forward, he can join in the attack, creating 3 v 2.
Take out players 1 & 4 and put in fullbacks and wingers.

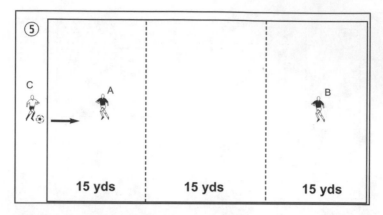

Player 'C' starts on the end line and dribbles into zone 1, trying to get past defender 'A'

If 'A' steals the ball, 'A' tries to dribble past 'C', and over the end line.

If 'C' manages to get by 'A', 'C' continues through zone 2 and tries to beat 'B' over the end line.

If 'B' steals it, he takes on player 'A' who has been waiting in zone 1.

Focus on:

Attackers:

Try to unbalance defender.

Attack at pace, try to keep facing the defender.

Change pace and direction.

Defenders:

Be positive and stand your ground. Force the attacker to beat you with ability. Know when to tackle.

Variations:

Allow defender 'A' to chase 'C' into zone 2 if beaten. 'C' must then hold 'A' off while at the same time moving towards taking on 'B'. This also doesn't allow 'C' to give up once beaten, teaching him to recover 'goal side'.

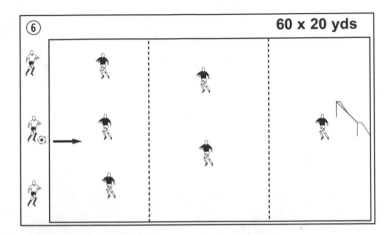

'Dribblers' try to dribble through the three zones occupied by the defenders.

Defenders must stay in their zones, and try to kick any ball that is dribbled through out of bounds.

'Dribblers' go three at a time. If a dribbler gets his ball knocked out, the next dribbler in line may go right away.

As soon as the 'dribbler' in front leaves the zone, the next 'dribbler' can also go.

After beating the last defender, the 'dribbler' must shoot the ball into the goal to get a point for his team.

Focus on:

Good dribbling technique.

Look for an opening... perhaps sending a teammate in early to act as a decoy, then when the defense opens up, take that chance to penetrate.

Variations:

Put a 'FREE ZONE' between each zone shown. The free zone can be 5 yards wide.

Once the dribbler gets in the free zone, he can rest before taking on the next defender.

You can also have people that make it into the free zone, leave their ball and assist the next person to try to get past the defender by passing.

Clever Clogs

Set Pieces

The outcome of a match can be decided on a team's ability and creativity at set pieces.

There is no better feeling as player or coach than when a set piece results in a goal. When set pieces work it shows people that you have been practicing, and have been inventive in your training, and every time you get a set piece the opposition is wondering what your team is going to do next.

If you are inventive and unpredictable you will catch the opposition cold and there will be more chance of your set piece working.

Set pieces are a great way to gain an advantage on the opposition and can mean the difference between winning and losing.

When practicing your set pieces you must ensure that the whole team knows what is going on. If there is one player who doesn't know, the play could be spoiled, so make sure every player understands what is going on.

If you are working on a set piece that involves a small number of players you can practice the drill and then bring in the players who have been doing other training and use them as the opposition.

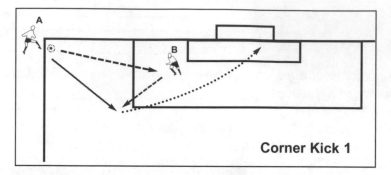

Corner Kick 1

Player B walks from the side of the 18 yard box towards the near post. He turns quickly to receive a pass from player A.
Player A moves to a shooting position and player B passes into his/her path.
Player A hits the target.

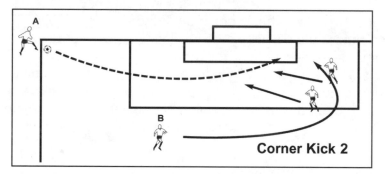

Corner Kick 2

Player B makes a bending run to the far post. As Player B begins to run, Player A strikes the ball, lofting it to the far post area. All other players run toward the near post in order to clear out the defenders from the far post.

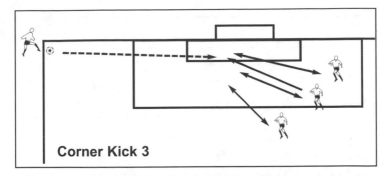

Corner Kick 3

All the attackers run to the near post but the player taking the corner fakes it and doesn't kick the ball.
The attackers turn and walk away from corner taker.
One of the attackers turns quickly and attacks near post.
The player taking the corner crosses the ball to the near post.

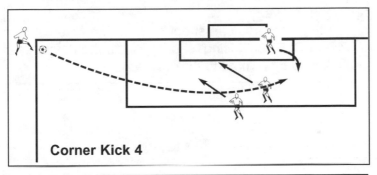

Corner Kick 4

Put one player standing on the far post. The full back will mark that player.
All the other players attack the near post.
The player on the far post peels off the full back who will stay marking the post.
The player taking the corner passes to the man on the far post for him to score.

GET PLAYERS TO USE HAND SIGNALS FOR EACH SET PIECE.

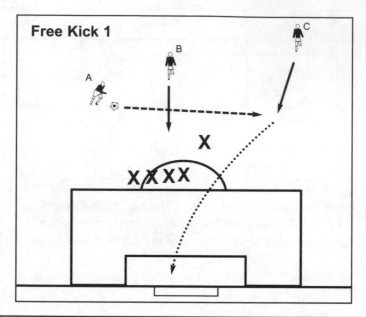

Player A taps ball to the on running Player B, who fakes the shot and allows the ball to run past so that on running Player C can shoot on net. The faked shot by Player B, if convincing, should freeze the defense and allow C more time to pick his target.

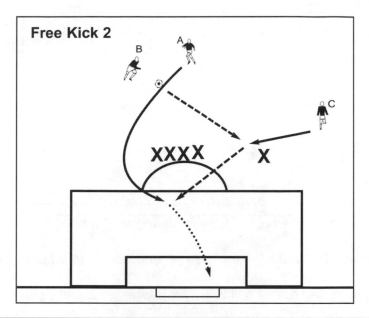

Free Kick 2

Players A and B are next to the ball. Player A runs
over the ball and around the wall. Player B passes the
ball to Player D who has made a horizontal run toward
the wall. Player D passes to Player A running behind
the wall.

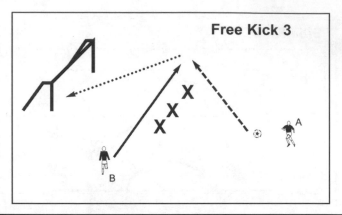

Free Kick 3

Player A lines up as though he is going to blast the free kick.
Player B walks behind the wall and stands in an open body position.
Player A passes ball to player B who shoots at goal.

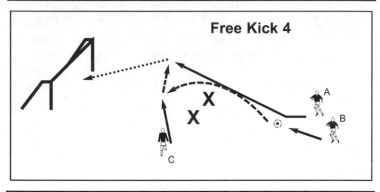

Free Kick 4

Player A fakes a shot and runs past the wall.
Player B chips the ball over the wall to player C who passes to oncoming player A, who shoots at goal.

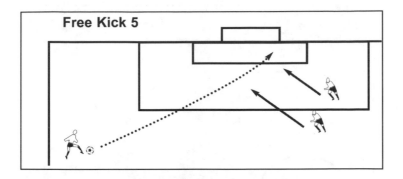

Free Kick 5

When you have a free kick from a wide position, get your players to whip the ball in to the far post.
The forwards attack the ball.
If any of the forwards or defenders miss the ball it is possible that the ball will go straight in, because the goalkeeper is in two minds.
Get your players to practice on their own hitting the far post head height, then bring in the players required.

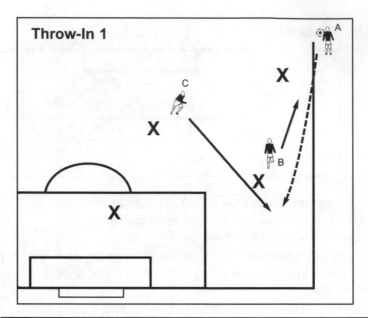

Throw-In 1

Player B runs toward Player A. Player A throws the ball over Player B's head to Player C who runs   behind Player B down the line.
Player C crosses the ball for the forwards to score.

Signals are not needed on the throw-ins. It is the players' creativity and ability to read a situation that can make a set play from a throw-in.
Throw-ins are just as important as a pass.

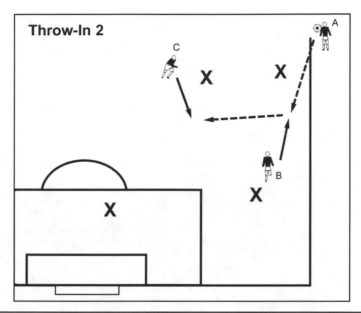

Throw-In 2

Player B runs hard toward Player A. Player A throws the ball to Player B's feet. Player B passes the ball (one-touch) to Player C running into space.

Throw-ins should be part of your training program. Make sure the players understand the importance of keeping possession from a throw-in.

Sample Training Session

Passing and Possession

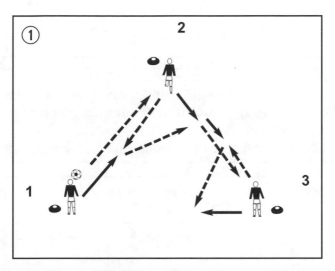

2 Players at each cone.
Player 1 passes on the ground to player 2 and fol-
lows his pass. Player 2 touches the ball back to
Player 1 and runs towards player 3.
Player 1 passes back into player 2's path. Player 2
then starts the same combination with player 3, and
so on. Go the opposite way.

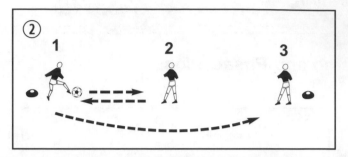

Player 1 passes on the ground to player 2, who touches the ball back. Player 1 then plays a long ball to player 3. Player 2 turns and plays the same combination with player 3.
Concentrate on precise passing and technique.

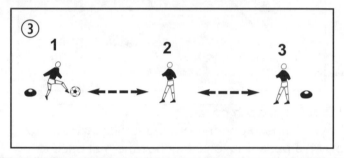

Players on the outside have a ball. Player 2 receives pass from player 1 and passes directly back, turns and receives pass from player 3.
Change the players around and then add a player in the middle.
Each inside player then turns to receive a pass from the opposite side.

Defending

The game is played with one goal and the team defending that goal plays possession. The team defending also has one or two more players than the team attacking.

The defending team plays two touch, while the attackers play unlimited touches.

Play for ten minutes and change the teams around. Count how many goals are scored by the attacking team and how many continuous passes are made by the team defending.

The team with five players has two touches.

The team with four players has unlimited touches.

Focus on:
Defending Team:
Communication.
First touch.
Decision.
Movement.
Attacking Team:
Pressure.
Scoring.

After this let the players play a game on two goals.

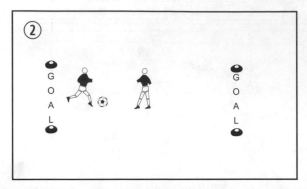

Players work in twos. The player with the ball passes to his opponent who tries to dribble across the line. If he succeeds he scores a point. Work for 10 minutes.

Same as above but now each player has to defend the two gates on his side. The player with the ball has to try to dribble through the cones.
Focus on:
Stay close to the player with the ball.
React to changes - stay flexible.

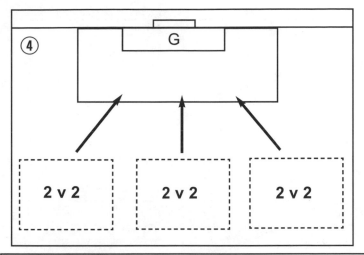

Three 2 v 2 play one after the other.
The object of the exercise is for the 2 attackers to get past the defenders and score.

⑤

Play a game with equal sides.
Each player is assigned a player from the other team to man mark.
When a player scores, his marker must perform 5 push-ups.
Depending on ability, play two touch.

Team Spirit

Team spirit is a continuous process, both on and off the pitch.

When you hear the term 'team spirit' you tend to think of the players. But in fact, you must look at the coaches and committee members as well. Everyone must pull together and be positive in building team spirit.

Much depends on the individual and his attitude and personality, but if you have winners with character in your squad, the way they behave will rub off on the rest of the team.

Team spirit is vital in building success so as a coach you must always be positive and honest.

Every coach should have objectives and rules for his team to follow and must never drift away from them. If you keep changing rules for certain players then people will quickly realize that you have favorites. These things will damage team spirit.

If you work towards your objective, you will realize that there are a lot of ups and downs. When games are lost you will get coaches blaming just the players, but when games are won some coaches claim the victory for themselves. The basic principle is that we all win and we all lose.

Raising your voice to players depends on the situation and the way it is said. The trick is to choose the right moment. The more you yell the less effect it has.

Last but not least we must consider the atmosphere. The game is about winning, but also it is about enjoyment. If enjoyment is not part of your training or playing, you can forget good results. Team spirit will be automatic when people feel good about what they are doing.

Players are going to make mistakes but so are coaches, the important thing is to learn from them.

Also available from Reedswain:

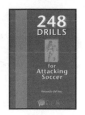

Also available from Reedswain:

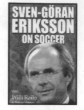